Books by Fran Stewart

The Biscuit McKee Mystery Series:

> *Orange as Marmalade*
> *Yellow as Legal Pads*
> *Green as a Garden Hose*
> *Blue as Blue Jeans*
> *Indigo as an Iris*
> *Violet as an Amethyst*
> *Gray as Ashes*
>
> *Red as a Rooster*
> *Black as Soot*
> *Pink as a Peony*
> *White as Ice*

A Slaying Song Tonight

The ScotShop Mysteries:

> *A Wee Murder in My Shop*
> *A Wee Dose of Death*
> *A Wee Homicide in the Hotel*

Poetry:

> *Resolution*

For Children:

> *As Orange As Marmalade/*
> *Tan naranja como Mermelada*
> (a bilingual book)

Non-Fiction:

> *From The Tip of My Pen: a workbook for writers*
> *BeesKnees #1: A Beekeeping Memoir (#1 of 6 volumes)*
> *BeesKnees #2: A Beekeeping Memoir (#2 of 6 volumes)*
> *BeesKnees #3: A Beekeeping Memoir (#3 of 6 volumes)*
> *BeesKnees #4: A Beekeeping Memoir (#4 of 6 volumes)*
> *BeesKnees #5: A Beekeeping Memoir (#5 of 6 volumes)*
> *BeesKnees #6: A Beekeeping Memoir (#6 of 6 volumes)*
> *Clear as Mud*
> *Clearly Me*
> *Crystal Clear*

Resolution

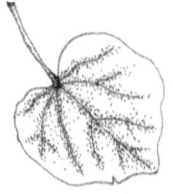
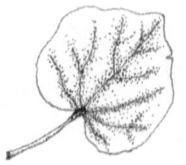

Fran Stewart

Resolution

1st edition: © 2006 Fran Stewart

All rights reserved. No part of this book may be used or reproduced in any manner whatsoever without written permission from the author, except by a reviewer who may quote brief passages in a review.

Illustrations by Diana Alishouse

ISBN: 978-1-951368-49-4

This book was printed in the United States of America.

Published by
My Own Ship Press
PO Box 490153
Lawrenceville GA 30049

myownship@icloud.com
franstewart.com

My Gratitude List:

Miss Helen Johnson, my seventh grade English teacher, who put up with my first efforts and even encouraged me.

Dr. Marie J. Robinson, Professor of Speech at Illinois Wesleyan University in the mid-sixties, who exposed me to more poems and poetic forms than I would have found on my own.

Jenny Sadre-Orafai, the editor of my poems, who wouldn't let me get away with anything less than my best, and who knew how to coax it out of me.

Introduction

My history with poetry goes back to childhood, when I had teachers who had the time to introduce us to timeless poems. I have loved the sweep of words ever since, and have learned to appreciate widely different poetic forms, from the exquisitely controlled structures of sonnets to the seemingly imprecise precision of free verse. I learned that I could read a poem out loud and glory in the sound, and that I could study line length and meter and rhyme schemes till my eyes crossed, but if the rhythm and the right sound and the exact words weren't there, it just wasn't poetry.

Part of the fun of poetry is its exploration of the fine nuances of the English language. I love English. I'm one of those incurable phonophiles—sometimes I read a thesaurus out loud for the sheer fun of it. Poetry leads one farther down the path of word-loving. This collection of poems is my addition to that path.

Fran Stewart
From my house by a creek
on the back side of Hog Mountain, Georgia
October, 2006

Table of Contents

Page

11	Conversation with Her
13	Inch of Air
15	Nothing New Here
17	Lines Composed Beside *Walden*
19	Inheritance
21	Water Fountain (1994 and 2005)
23	What Feeds Us
25	Amateur's View of a Professional
27	When I Dream of Fires
29	Gift
31	Resolution
33	Your Hand on My Shoulder
35	Both Moons
37	So What?
39	Before I Wake
41	Two Canadians, One American Killed While Fleeing Hotel Fire
43	Weather Forecast
45	My Father's Rocks
47	Touch-Typing
49	Lava
51	Your Bouquet / My Bouquet
53	Baloney: On Considering the Collective Process
55	Gravity's Work

Conversation with Her

Two brooding spiders concentered on their webs
in one tight corner of the world,
each strand a gray hair,
the cobwebs of their years.

She plucks a string—loud laughter,
boisterous, full of myriad eggs hatched to spider babies
floating up on stray breezes and sunwarmed currents.
No self-respecting spider, the naturalists tell us,
is ever trapped by the mucous strands
of her own web.

Are we, though, pulling horses together
joining them, each to each,
in cosmic webbings
of some other's design, but sometimes
with strands of our own music?

Are we the victims of the fire
or the fuel that lights the way
for those who spin their webs in other corners,
but in the same room,
who heard our music and spun accordingly?

After our talk I pull back together
my silk colon, my diaphragm,
my liver, and my still-pulsating heart,
rein in my four percherons, and
twist up my skein of gray webbing,
spilling all in such profusion,
weaving so long a tale.

Yes. I flung gray webs across the table
where we sat over tea and recollections,
eating the dead and living flies decorating our coffeecake,
thinking they were raisins, sun-grown, sun-dried,
nutrition and dessert all at once.

Let's dig up to the daylight greenhouse corner
and spin a new web,
meet again to dissect it,
eat our flies in public,
and not care what grasshoppers think.

Inch of Air
for David Cavanagh

Taking a book from your shelf
and opening it to your bookmark—
a plain white sheet—is dangerous.

That inch of air in *cross/cut*
cut me across
and left me bleeding.

Why do you leave
such weapons lying around?
Why do I pick them up?

Nothing New Here

Don't ever take food into the bathroom.
That was the rule,
not to be violated, but I did.
It was a piece of white cake
on a white napkin,
and my underpants were white.
But not there, not where I couldn't look.
But I did. And saw the unspeakable.
Lunging with my underpants still halfway down,
slacks pulled up to hide my shame,
I hid the white cake on its white napkin
tucked them into my dresser's jumbled top,
then trundled back
through the bathroom door, Charlie Chaplinesque,
to sit and rearrange myself and call out, "Mama."
She didn't see the cake.

Eight years later, she didn't see my new cake, either.
A fragrant, musky, thirty-six-year-old mouthful
filled with walnuts and dates and seeded figs
and passion fruit I had never tasted before.
I hid that cake, too.
I still had to rearrange myself before I called.
"Hello, Mama. . . . No, there's nothing new here."

Lines Composed Beside *Walden*

What right had you,
a squatter in my field,
to build your house
by my own Walden Pond?
Did you think I'd given you leave
by a word or look
to tramp my grass, fell my pines,
and dig your cellar through my bank?
Where did you cart my sand,
my pebbles, my former foundation?
And what, besides rubble, did you leave behind?

Inheritance

Rocking beneath Grandma's pecan trees,
I sat with him discussing wisdom of the ages.
He held a black book,
its leaves as frail and dry as hands.
Almost every word was underlined in red.
We spoke a while that day.
Other times, we didn't talk.
He was seventy,
with a neck like the chicken my grandmother
hacked off for Sunday dinner.
Mother hinted that Grandma had her own story to tell,
but didn't tell it except to the womenfolk,
and I wasn't a womanfolk yet.

He held his arms close to his side,
protecting his godliness
with elbows I never saw
because of long-sleeved blue shirts
(except on Sunday of course,
when shirts and reputations were white).

He never smoked.
It was ungodly, he said. Un-god-ly.
That black book he held
held his lists of what was godly and what was un.
It held lists of children born.
I was in it, though I never saw my name,
not wanting to know which column he put me in.
It was all my fault, he told me each time.

In his seventy years he tallied more
of the ungodly than the opposite.
Uncle Daniel bears scars of his righteous retribution.
I look at my grandfather's rocking chair,
the one I inherited.
The left armrest has *J. Dani* crudely carved in it.
That was when Grandpa caught him.
My father's eyes gleamed
when he told of John Daniel being dragged
out behind the tool shed—
where I had to put
the flea powder on the barn cats each summer.

They squirmed and yowled as I sprinkled
the white, white powder in childish abandon.
It sifted through their eyes and nostrils.
In just such a way, John Daniel must have hated
the white hot godliness raining down on his bare back.

Grandmother's pecan trees offered no conclusion.
They shaded, instead, an old man,
and a little girl, there at his behest,
hugging her own questions,
bent over her own knees.

Water Fountain (1994 and 2005)

All my gray-haired wisdom
Seems bound up in this:
       Don't lean over
       a water fountain
       before you see
       how high it squirts.

All my gray-haired wisdom
Leaps up to cry:
       Check out every water fountain;
       glory in the stream.
       Look!
       See how high it squirts!

Resolution

What Feeds Us

Although your tree
and mine
are one,
your vision
is not
my vision.

You see leaves.
I, crenelated bark.

You see the way the tree reaches up
for air and rain.
I sense the delving,
the tunneling branch of roots,
clawing their way
past earthworms and beetles,
searching blind-eyed for wisp of wet,
for ache of sustenance,
for the chance to hold
tight to underlying rocks,
draining their minerals,
drinking deep from the belly of our mother.

You see sunlight on leaves.
I see gossamer undersides of those same leaves,
their veins stretched with hammering pulse of sap.

Amateur's View of a Professional

Peg, like a black & white photo of herself
    white polka dots on black skirt
        hair a touch of sepia
Juxtaposition of umbrella and her camera
    poke-flash, poke-flash
        lighting up her field

Not my chin.
    Don't photograph my chin.
But that's the only way to get
    the umbrella in the background.
What an umbrella
    with the lightning underneath it.
Where is your rain, Peg?
    Or do you, Zeus-like, dispense with the rain
        and use only lightning?
Too much laughter for rain here, anyway.
    Her subject relaxes
        and poses
            and points
                and smiles.
Great, you say.
    Wonderful, you say.
        Perfect, you say.
She blooms and turns into
    the rainbow your umbrella was seeking,
        the one your lightning bolts
            wanted to illuminate.

You hike your polka-dots
    to straddle a heavy chain barrier.
Used to do sports photos, you say.
    Got run over by a football team.
        Broke my back.
            This is safer.

But still, there's all that lightning.
    And you with two black-box lightning-rods
        strung around your neck.
Peg, did you ever wonder what would happen if
    the lightning started coming from *you*—
if you could touch your ear instead of that button
    to make the flash happen?
You could touch your toe to the ground
    to ground yourself
and become the flame that would light all your pictures
    and reflect all your subjects
        and carry all your images
            from here to Olympus
                and back again to the darkroom.

When I Dream of Fires

I dream destruction.
I awaken
Wet and cold,
my heart rides
the loop-de-loop
and leaves me
behind.

When I dream of your fire,
I dream creation
and I awaken
wet and warm,
my heart rides
the loop-de-loop
and takes me along.

Gift

My words on gray paper
written with my hand
and a gold pen.

Resolution

The night my mother died
I sang and read and prayed;
I knitted as I thought about my life
And saw the fraying strands that joined me
                with that woman lying on the bed.

The night my mother died
I listened to her breathe,
Then set aside my knitting and my book;
I called my sister, moved my chair across the room,
                up to my mother's bed.

I took her hand in mine
And eased my other hand,
Light as I could, straight on her struggling heart.
So frail—the fluttering of a dozen finches
                brushed against my fingertips.

The night my mother died
I held her crumpled hand;
No stranger—that—to me. I recognized
Her fingers—gnarled, tight-jointed, twisted,
                frozen in an agonized refrain.

I worked my fingers in.
Her fist was closed. So tight.
So barricaded, as her heart had been.
The clock above her bed struck one.
                The finches shook. Her breath was hard to hear.

And when my mother died,
She took a final breath;
She held it, arched her back and groaned, and then
She sang her final song, a long slow sigh
              that lifted her, and she was gone.

The finches hadn't heard.
For ninety years they'd beat
Their wings; for ninety seconds more they tried.
They fluttered, faltered, strove to fly,
              and settled, finally, folding in their wings.

The night my mother died,
Her hand, so tight, so closed,
Opened, and I held a baby's hand,
Soft and supple. Liver-spotted,
              but—somehow—new.

The gift my mother gave
To me the night she died
Was a deep, strong, heart-committed knowing
That I will never close my fist and wait
              for Death to come and open it.

Resolution

Your Hand on My Shoulder

Lightning
without
thunder.

Both Moons

Tonight I lay beside the lake
And, dear, watched both moons.
The first sat, starched in her petticoat of clouds,
And little changed, except to slowly fall;
She held her not-born in her meager lap
And tried to promise birth.

But the other moon
Was marriage, parent, child.
My littlest finger, dipped into the lake
(As I would yours had been)
Made a match of moon and lake.
Made them one, then two, then one,
Then two, then one, then two.

So What?

So what if you're gone?
This leaf in my hand
holds the promise
of the tree
under which
we stood.

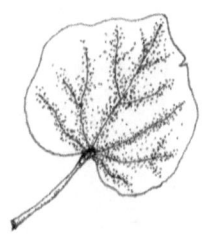

Before I Wake

I loved to sleep
when I was young.
I dreaded waking.
But then someone taught me that ghastly prayer,
"If I should die before I wake . . ."
What if, what if, what if?

And then, there came the day I knew
there was truth to learn:
If I should die before
I wake to the possibilities of my life,
what would I miss?

Let me live, truly live, before I sleep,
and certainly before I die.
Let me wake, wake, wake before I sleep.

Resolution

Two Canadians, One American Killed While Fleeing Hotel Fire

Fleeing—
is wrong.
The knots you formed
held.
Your wife would have been safe,
had she followed you
down the bedsheet highway
you built.
You tested it for her
with your heavier weight.
The knots held.
Your hands, though?

Thirty-two feet
per second
squared,
the rate of acceleration
of a falling body
due to gravity.
My physics teacher was referring,
      of course,
to an iron ball
or a feather (in a glass jar
to eliminate the possible action
of updrafts).
Let's say your hands
slipped
at the fourth floor.
Let's say ten feet per floor.
Forty feet.

Fran Stewart

Eight feet more than a second
you had, to flail and fear.
Or, did you fold your wings,
an eagle   *soar*
  plummeting   *and*
    to earth   *again*
      to grasp death,   *lift*
        your prey,   *and*
          in your talons,

Weather Forecast

That wind,
breaking branches,
is nothing.

This wind,
your breath on my hair,
is something.

My Father's Rocks

We always walk on jewels, but seldom see
The shimmering heart within the smallest stone.
Our feet, unthinking, stumble, stride, or stand
On quartz or geodes, yet we feel alone.

My father used to polish rocks. He'd scoop
Handfuls of pebbles, slip them in an urn,
Crank the lid down, tumble them for days,
Then spill sparkling fires, and we would learn

What *we* saw dull, he'd known was fire,
Volcanic, bursting forth from underground,
Then moved by grinding glacial weight to sit
Beside tiger's eyes my father found.

Now, through my feet, I feel (when I stand apart)
One unassuming rock—my father's heart.

Touch-Typing

You sit at a keyboard
and touch type.

Lucky keys.

Lava

All legs and tongue—
the color of just-crusting lava—
brown, burnt-orange, copper.
Upside down in my lap
stretching to lick my chin.
All legs and tongue and love
bundled in silky rumpled coat
choosing me before I knew how to choose her.
Testing the bounds of obedience
—who's training whom?
Why has she claimed me when I
have not returned the favor?

All those years,
walks,
ears flapping,
trying to catch us.
Then, soon, erupting past,
around us, almost *through*.
She ran in circles,
with me her chosen center,
pulled her heart out on the sled,
climbed in laps without permission,
always all legs and tongue.

And then her stomach torsed.
And the vet took her ash and breathed in the breath of life
and *saved* her.
So,
for a year I cleaned up vomit.
Vomit—here and there—

like cookies not yet baked.
And then I am expecting, vomiting myself.
Get up, throw up,
clean up her vomit, flush mine.
Can't she die and stop this?

When she died
there were more legs than anything else
and her tongue, rattling, swelling in her throat,
drooping to the floor as she lay
at the foot of the stairs
—hard cold floor
February: frozen ground and inconvenience.
When she choked
on that last percussive sound of death,
I recoiled from her, from It, from what I feared,
Then threw myself on her—
no, not her—not the blarney,
not the molten lava streaking by,
not that. No, just dead red fur
with nothing left to flop or drip.

I hauled her hardened lava to the Humane Society.
I, who chose to leave her with strangers
when I should have presented her as a burnt offering,
my Vesuvius of Flapping Ears—
I, who refused the duties of the living,
who paid the strangers my thirty pieces of silver
(Your donation is greatly appreciated)
to be spared the bother of a winter disposal—
I, who chose to let strangers sweep up her ash,
when I should have bound a remnant of her hair
into a necklace, a talisman,
a shield against the volcanic forces that deny love.

Resolution

Your Bouquet

One rose for romance,
a sprig of baby's breath for sentiment,
a violet for spring,
one maple leaf for fall.

My Bouquet

For romance, rue.
For sentiment, a pungent marigold.
Fresh dill for summer's heat.
For winter, three dried grasses
      limned with frost.

Resolution

Baloney: On Considering the Collective Process

Scurry, scurry, twitch your crumb-coated whiskers
As you pause to clean off debris
From this fifteenth confabulation of the day.
So important, so important, run this way and that.
Check and recheck the columns
Of figures. Go figure. Then check
The checkers and the ones who check them.
We must consense, we must agree
We must discuss it all
All
All
All
All is baloney until we have digested it
And then it comes out.

Gravity's Work
for Lori H.

Twelve years ago I would have lost face
over this hole in my nylons;
I even carried extras in the car.
Twelve years ago, I carefully ironed each shirt
depending on steam and pressure to erase
what wearing and washing had put there.
Now, I hang each shirt
straight out of the dryer
and let gravity relax the wrinkles.

Twelve years ago, I ironed my face each morning.
Good morning, Fran, this face won't do.
Natural, subtle, the real me, ready-to-go
after only eleven and a half minutes.
Until the day you said offhandedly,
> "I wouldn't mind experimentation
> for medical reasons.
> A rabbit's life for a child's
> seems justifiable, somehow.
> But for cosmetics? It seems
> so—somehow—silly."

Good morning, Fran, this face won't do.
But, for once, I argue with that
mirror mirror on the wall,
behind it the countless reflections
of beasts—not mute—
> speaking *my* language
> waiting, caged, for the White Coat
> and muffled shoes

>   to spread my private parts
>   and scrape the swab across
>   my cringing membranes.
> An impersonal violation, in the interests of knowledge.
> How can any blush be subtle when bought at such a price?
> What need have I—really—of mascara
> to lengthen any lash?
> How can a history of bunny eyes blinded for me
> add to my stature as a god-forgive-me woman?
> Now I hang my face out of the drying
> and let gravity relax the wrinkles.

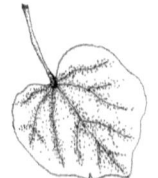
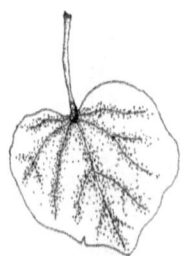
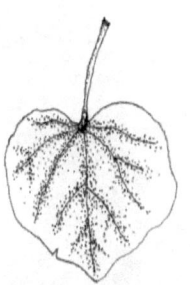

Index of first lines

Page

49	All legs and tongue
21	All my gray-haired wisdom
23	Although your tree
15	Don't ever take food into the bathroom
41	Fleeing
51	For romance, rue
27	I dream destruction
39	I loved to sleep
33	Lightning
29	My words on gray paper
51	One rose for romance
25	Peg, like a black & white photo of herself
19	Rocking beneath Grandma's pecan trees
53	Scurry, scurry, twitch your crumb-coated whiskers
37	So what if you're gone?
13	Taking a book from your shelf
43	That wind
31	The night my mother died
35	Tonight I lay beside the lake
55	Twelve years ago I would have lost face
11	Two brooding spiders concentered on their webs
45	We always walk on jewels, but seldom see
17	What right had you
47	You sit at a keyboard

www.ingramcontent.com/pod-product-compliance
Lightning Source LLC
Chambersburg PA
CBHW030139100526
44592CB00011B/965